Agile Project Management

Step-by-Step Guide to Agile Project Management

(Agile Principles, Agile Software Development, DSDM Atern, Agile Project Scope)

Jason Bennett & Jennifer Bowen

Table of Contents

INTRODUCTION 6

CHAPTER 1 - AGILE VALUES AND PRINCIPLES 8

CHAPTER 2 - WHO CAN USE AGILE? 20

CHAPTER 3 - AGILE SOFTWARE DEVELOPMENT

TECHNIQUES 28

CHAPTER 4 - DSDM ATERN.. 38

CHAPTER 5 - ROLES IN DSDM PROJECT MANAGEMENT

.... 44

CHAPTER 6 - MANAGING SCOPE AND PROCUREMENT

WITH AGILE 50

CONCLUSION.. 58

Introduction

While the concept of using incremental improvements in developing software have been around as early as the late 1950s, the Agile PMS was initially deliberated in great detail during the 1970s in a paper published by William Royce, which discussed developing large software systems.

Fast forward to the year 2001, the 17 pioneers of the Agile PMS came up with what's now known as the Agile Manifesto that formally declared Agile's key values and principles help guide software developers use a people-centered and iterative approach to doing their jobs. Agile refers to a method of managing projects, which features the use of brief development cycles or "sprints" in order to center on continuous improvement when developing services or products.

The Agile project management system or Agile PMS was borne out of frequent cancellations of many projects resulting from the enormous delays in providing technology or software solutions for the needs or preferences of customers that were suffered by many businesses in the past.

To be more specific, the rapid pace at which customers' needs were changing and the slow development and delivery of software solutions to such needs, which were mostly based on the Waterfall model, made the eventual delivery of solutions obsolete.

This was because during the very slow development times, the needs and preferences of customers changed so much that by the time the solutions were finally developed and delivered, they were no longer relevant to the customers' new needs and preferences.

Another aggravating factor was the fact that software development back in the day wasn't as flexible or agile when it comes to meeting customers' changing needs as they are now.

This was the case until the year 2000 when 17 of the most prominent personalities in the software development industry, which included among others Alistair Cockburn, Arie van Bennekum, Ward Cunningham, Kent Beck, and Jon Kern, got together and joined forces in Oregon.

The meeting would then be repeated in 2001, this time in Utah at the Snowbird ski resort. On that 2nd meeting, the Agile Manifesto was born, together with its twin sibling, the 12 Agile Principles. The Manifesto enumerates the 4 main values of Agile. This is the Agile Manifesto:

> *We are uncovering better ways of developing software by doing it and helping others do it. Through this work we have come to value:*

> — *Individuals and interactions over processes and tools;*
> — *Working software over comprehensive documentation;*
> — *Customer collaboration over contract negotiation; and*
> — *Responding to change over following a plan.*

That is, while there is value in the items on the right, we value the items on the left more.

Chapter 1 - Agile Values And Principles

Systems can only be consistently effective if they have a solid set of values and principles underlying them. And more importantly, such values and principles need to be practiced during implementation. The following are the key values and principles underlying the Agile project management system.

Agile Values

Individuals And Interactions Over Processes And Tools

The Agile project management system puts a premium on people over everything else. Why? It's because business needs don't respond to people but people respond to business needs, as well as drive the process of development.

The 17 Agile pioneers recognized that the likelihood of meeting customers' needs is very low if the development is driven primarily by tools or processes because in such cases, project management teams aren't able to respond very well to changes.

One area where project management teams driven mostly by processes and tools are inferior to people driven teams is communications. In teams that are driven by processes and tools, communications need to have specific types of content and are scheduled.

But in people-driven teams, communications can be fluid and can be done whenever concerns arise - and this allows teams to respond faster to changing clients' needs.

Working Software Over Comprehensive Documentation

In the past, documentation of product development and delivery took a lot of time - time that could've been spent on more important matters. This was because of the bureaucracy involved in documentation, which required approval for each important aspect such as technical specs, requirements, and prospectus, as well as documents related to interface design, plans for software testing, and even plans for documenting the plans!

As you can see, the amounts of documentation required for software development back in the day can be so insane and anal that with the documentation processes alone, software development can take on a turtle's pace and were often the reason for many delays.

While the Agile PMS is not about eliminating documentation, it dramatically reduces, the amount of documentation needed, particularly the amount of time it takes from the whole development time.

Agile streamlines the documentation process in such a way that it provides just the right amount of documentation software developers need to finish what they need to do without having to get so caught up in unproductive minutiae.

Documents prepared using the Agile PMS are prepared as user "stories," which is enough for any software developer to start creating new functions on old ones. Make no mistake about it, Agile PMS views documentation as very important but not at the expense of being able to develop software and deliver them on time.

Customer Collaboration Over Contract Negotiation

Negotiations refer to when customers and product managers thrash out details of software delivery. It also includes changing existing details where necessary. Using primarily a Waterfall-based methodology, customers give developers their requirements in such great detail just before the software development process commences. When the process is completed, clients also participate in the post development process. But the problem is this: clients are left out of the middle process, which is the actual software development process.

Not so with an Agile PMS. The manifesto portrays a client who's not detached from the development process but is engaged, i.e., collaborates with developers all throughout the process of developing software, including the middle part or the actual development process itself.

By being involved during the software development process itself, clients help make it easier for developers to meet their needs.

With an Agile-based project management system, end-users can collaborate at periodic times during the development of software only or be part of the whole process from start to finish and attend each and every team meeting to make sure that all of their needs are met by the finished product.

Responding To Changes Over Following Plans

Changes were considered as nothing more than unnecessary expenses under software development methods prior to Agile and hence, should be avoided as much as possible.

This was because of the belief that software development plans should be very elaborate and detailed, having a highly identified set of characteristics, where practically everything is considered as "top priority."

But not so with the Agile PMS, which allows for shifting from iteration of software to another, where new features can be included in the succeeding iterations.

Agile PMS proponents believe that changes aren't unnecessary expenses, but opportunities to make projects much better because changes don't reduce value, i.e., expenses, but instead add to it.

A concept called Method Tailoring best illustrates Agile's favorable treatment of change. Based on An Agile Information Systems Development Method, Method Tailoring can be thought of as:

> *A process or capability in which human agents determine a system development approach for a specific project situation through responsive changes in, and dynamic interplays between, contexts, intentions, and method fragments.*

In essence, Agile-based software development methods allow software development teams to change the development process to make it fit them instead of them having to fit themselves to the process.

The 12 Principles Of Agile

1. The highest priority should always be customer satisfaction, which can be accomplished by fast and continuous delivery;

2. Developers must welcome changing environments regardless of the software development process stage in order to give clients an advantage over their competitors;

3. Services or products must be delivered more frequently;

4. Developers must closely collaborate with project stakeholders every day;

5. All team members and stakeholders must always be motivated in order to get the most outcomes from projects, with software development teams being provided everything needed for successful completion of projects, including high levels of trust, so that they may be able to accomplish all goals;

6. As much as possible, meetings must be done face-to-face because meeting this way is the most efficient and effective way to successfully complete projects;

7. The best way to measure a project's success is the final working product;

8. Agile processes, i.e., ones where stakeholders and software development teams can keep a continuous and constant pace should be used to accomplish sustainable developments;

9. Continuous focus on proper design and technical excellence enhances agility;

10. One of the most important elements for success is simplicity;

11. For developing the best project designs and architectures and to meet clients' requirements, self-organizing teams are best suited;

12. Teams should use regularly timed fine-tuning behaviors or activities to continue improving efficiency.

Adopting An Agile Project Management Methodology

While Agile was initially created for software development projects, it can be used - and indeed, it's now being used - in many different types of projects that aren't software in nature.

This is because of the methodology's high efficiency and premium on collaboration between clients and businesses. According to a survey conducted by Version One, the Agile project management system's adoption rates across different industries are as follows:

- Software: 23%
- Financial Services: 14%
- Professional Services: 12%
- Insurance: 6%
- Healthcare: 6%
- Government: 5%
- Telecommunications: 4%
- Transportation: 4%
- Manufacturing: 4%

The Agile Delivery Framework: 5 Phases

The Agile PMS uses a 5-phase framework for delivering projects to clients, which aside from being very specific is also iterative and flexible. These phases include Envisioning, Speculating, Exploring, Adapting, and Closing.

Using the Agile PMS, projects iterate through the Speculation, Exploration, and Adaptation phases when a project or software's features are being finalized or when a specific timeline or criteria has been met.

The first phase of the Agile project delivery framework is Envisioning, which is the phase when initial planning for projects are completed, i.e., when the project's scope and vision are determined, and when a project charter is created. In this phase, the identities and roles of stakeholders are clarified and the development team's norms are established.

The second phase is the speculation phase, which is when decisions regarding what software features will be undertaken in an iteration are made. In a sense, this may be considered as an "incomplete" planning session, where it usually resembles educated guessing on the part of project teams because at this point, the necessary information for working on a project remains to be completed.

During this phase, project teams try to get a reasonable "guesstimate" as to how long each feature can be finished the following iteration and the time needed to achieve other pending milestones.

The third phase is exploration, which is the time when project teams work on finishing all agreed upon features for a specific iteration. The reasons why this phase is called "explore" or "exploration" is because Agile project teams literally explore ways on how to effectively implement a specific feature, i.e., make it work. During this phase, quality testing and stakeholder management is also performed.

The fourth phase is the adaptation or "adapt" phase, which is scheduled to proceed at a predetermined time. The reason for proceeding with this phase only after a specific time has lapsed is to give enough time for stakeholders and development teams to exchange crucial information or feedback that can help make the project successful.

Under this phase, results of the exploration phase are compared to the feature completion plans made in the speculation phase. The adaptation or adapt phase provides very good opportunities for development teams to make the necessary changes or adjustments prior to re-iterating to the speculation phase.

The last phase in the Agile PMS delivery framework is the closing or the close phase. This phase, which is only done once, can only proceed after the final pending iteration of a project has been successfully concluded. In this phase, development teams process any learnings from the just concluded project prior to being cleared to proceed with a new one.

Agile Performance Measurement

Any endeavor, including managing projects, need certain parameters by which to evaluate. And such parameters need to be objectively quantifiable because in the absence of such, it can be very challenging to effectively assess whether or not a project management system such as Agile is effective or not.

The following are measurements or parameters that can be used to evaluate how an Agile project was carried out:

1. Lead Time: Refers to the amount of time elapsed from the time the project started (coding) to the time it was produced (production);

2. Frequency of Deployment: Refers to the number of times a particular code was deployed;

3. Failed Deployment Percentage: The ratio of actual number of failed deployments or negative impacts to the total number of deployments for a specific code;

4. Mean Recovery Time: The average speed at which code deployment failures are remedied or fixed;

5. Customer Satisfaction: The percentage of issued tickets concerning issues or negative customer experiences with a specific code;

6. New User Volume Percentage: Increase in new user participation, in percentage form;

7. Bug Defects: Refers to the actual frequency of defects for every code deployment;

8. Availability: How much time the system was up without problems compared to total time;

9. Project Completion Rate: The number of completed projects during a specific investment time period, e.g., per quarter.

Why Agile Works Better

In the beginning, Agile was created primarily for software developers and their clients, the primary goal for which was to improve and streamline the software development process to enable the swift identification of and adjustment for defects and issues.

The Agile PMS gives software developers and teams a means by which to give their customers a much better product and in a timelier manner by using brief, iterative, and interactive sprints or sessions.

In today's highly digitized age, more and more businesses - both big and small - are shifting to a mostly digital work environment, for which the Agile project management system is a great fit.

The Agile PMS can help businesses who are shifting more and more to a digital working environment better manage individual projects as well as their organizations as a whole much, much better. It can help them make sure that processes and method alignments are implemented across the whole organization.

To be more specific, the Agile project management system can help make businesses even more flexible, productive, transparent, capable of higher quality products and services, capable of timely and consistent delivery of products and services, and capable of providing optimal satisfaction and engagement to all concerned stakeholders.

This means developers, teams, team leaders, and even customers can enjoy:

- Better and faster identification of defects and issues;
- Better capacity for adapting to and making the most out of changes;
- Better focus on customer's specific needs;
- Faster delivery and implementation of solutions;
- Maximized development activities;
- Maximum control over projects;
- More focused efforts leading to more successes;
- More frequent collaboration with and feedback from stakeholders;
- Simpler framework;
- Speedier project turnaround times; and
- Substantially reduced wastage of resources through increased efficiency.

Potential Issues With Agile

While the Agile project management system is a very efficient and effective way for businesses to deliver their products and services to their customers, both internal and external, it's not perfect. No system is. For one, Agile doesn't sit well with some types of projects, which necessitates due diligence before implementation or even consideration.

In particular, the Agile PMS will not work well with projects where the clients' goals are ambiguous, the project team's leader or members aren't capable of implementing the Agile PMS, or if the development team's members easily buckle under pressure.

Also, the Agile PMS tends to favor goals set by the software developers, the development teams, and the customers. However, it doesn't follow that it automatically puts a premium on the experience of end users.

What this means is that the Agile PMS may not work well with large and highly traditional businesses or organizations whose people, structure, and management are still highly rigid because the Agile system is one that's highly flexible and isn't as formal or rigid.

It may prove to be unproductive when dealing with customers who are too traditional and rigid in their ways.

Chapter 2 - Who Can Use Agile?

Agile is a highly specialized methodology to managing projects and as such, can't just be used or implemented by any person. A person who would want to use or implement Agile in his or her workplace needs 2 important things: key skills and certifications.

Key Skills

If you want to implement Agile well in your organization as a project manager, you'll need to possess these 6 crucial Agile-related skills:

1. A great amount of flexibility to be able to accept and deal with project changes as they happen so that risk and confusion brought about by such can be minimized;

2. Above-average organizational skills so you can prioritize the right things and keep things orderly;

3. Fast thinking and decision-making skills, especially when the circumstances surrounding projects change quickly;

4. Teaching and motivation skills for supporting and guiding project teams as they work on completing their projects successfully;

5. The ability to make sound judgments while under tremendous pressure, as well as the capacity to stay composed and calm in the midst of tremendous stress;

6. The capability to focus only on work that's important and essential and nothing more.

These 6 skills aren't the only ones you'll need to be able to successfully implement Agile in managing your organization's projects but having them will significantly boost your chances of being able to do so.

Agile Certifications

The massive success of the Agile PMS has practically revolutionized software development and the way managers manage projects. This has resulted in a massive increase in demand for information technology or I.T. professionals who have sufficient knowledge and experience with Agile and its many derivatives, which include Scaled Agile, Kanban, Scrum, and Lean.

Agile emphasizes iterative and incremental collaborations on projects between cross-functional teams, which is now done in many different types of organizations. This means one can't just be an average software developer or project manager in order to successfully implement it.

How can organizations looking for Agile managers to run their projects know whether or not the person they're considering hiring can do the job well?

And I think the better question to ask may be: How can you significantly increase your chances of being able to convince prospective employers to hire you as an Agile project manager? This is where Agile certifications come into play.

While the following Agile certifications aren't an ironclad evidence of ability and skill, they can provide organizations with more than enough information about your Agile-related capabilities and risks.

So if you're really serious about making a career out of the Agile project management system, I highly recommend giving any of these certifications a shot.

PMI-ACP

The Project Management Institute's (PMI) Agile Certified Practitioner (ACP) certification program is primarily for project managers in organizations who are either moving towards full adoption of Agile methodologies or are have already fully adapted it. This certification gives organizations to whom you'll be applying a high level of assurance that you have working experience in managing projects the Agile way and that you're acquainted with the various aspects of Agile methodologies such as Lean, Kanban, and Scrum, among others.

If you're a PMI-ACP certified project manager, you'll need to earn 30 PDUs or professional development units every 3 years just for you to continue remaining certified.

You can take the PMI-ACP certification exam either in paper or computerized form, which can set you back anywhere from $385 (paper test) to $495 (computerized test) if you're not yet a PMI member.

APMG International

This is an international organization that accredits project managers globally with several Agile-related certification programs.

The primary goal of APMG is to standardize project managers' abilities all over the world in terms of being able to implement the Agile methodologies for managing projects in organizations that need visibility, rigor, and standards within the framework of Agile. APMG offers 3 certification programs: Agile Program Management, Agile Project Management, and Dynamic Systems Development Method (DSDM), which is a vendor-neutral project delivery and management structure.

Depending on which certification program and exam you'll be taking, you can expect to invest between £218 ($293) to £330 ($443) to get certified.

Strategyex Certificate In Agile

This Agile certification comes in 2 variants: an Associate and a Master's Certificate in Agile practices. The Associate version will require you to finish 3 courses in a span of 2 years, with emphasis on your Agile-related skills and knowledge. The Master's version will require you to finish 7 courses within a span of 4 years in order to show your level of Agile expertise.

Only the Master's level certification will let you add the certification credential after your name. This certification program is conducted by an online learning group called TwentyEighty Strategy Execution (Strategyex) together with George Washington University.

Taking the Strategyex Certificate in Agile Certification can cost you around $1,645.

International Consortium For Agile - ICAgile

This comprehensive certification program provides expert training for all Agile methodologies, which include Kanban, eXtreme Programming (XP), and Scrum, among others. The ICAgile certification has 3 levels, which are Professional, Expert, and Master. This is to exhaustively assess a candidate's Agile-related working knowledge and skills. The certification costs $60 only.

Agile Certification Institute (ACI)

The ACI focuses on all areas of Agile project management across enterprises, which means it's not just limited to software development. The organization provides many Agile credentials and certifications, which cover among others Agile process improvement, Agile talent management and development, and Agile product and project management.

And more than just Agile enterprise certifications, ACI also provides certification for Scrum, Kanban, and Lean for Associates, Practitioners, Masters, and Owners. ACI offers each Agile course for $99.

Scaled Agile Academy

When the Agile methodology starts to be implemented in much bigger organizations, Agile project managers who have a very good knowledge and skills about scaling the implementation to a bigger framework become even more valuable. Also known as SAFe, the Scaled Agile Framework's course provides the necessary foundation skills and knowledge to be able to successfully implement the Lean/Agile system in much bigger organizations.

Scaled Agile Academy gives 5 types of certifications to help project managers show they're capable of implementing the Agile framework on a much bigger scale. These include The SAFe Program Consultant Trainer, The SAFe Program Consultant, The SAFe Agilist, The SAFe Practitioner, and The SAFe Product Manager/Product Owner certifications.

Each course will set you back around $995, where your first exam is free. Once you get certified, you'll have to pay $100 every year to renew your membership/certification.

Scrum Alliance

The most popular Agile methodology framework is Scrum, particularly when it comes to software development projects. Scrum Alliance is a top membership-based group for Scrum professionals, the goal of which is to support Scrum's widespread adoption and successful practice.

It offers 6 certifications for software development and information technology professionals, which include Certified Scrum Master, Certified Scrum Product Owner, Certified Scrum Developer, Certified Scrum Trainer, Certified Scrum Coach, and Certified Scrum Professional.

The program will set you back a considerable amount of money, $1,547 for each course, to be exact. And once you've been certified, there's an annual renewal fee of $250 you'll need to pay to stay certified.

Why Some Organizations Have Difficulty With Agile Adoption

As mentioned earlier, Agile isn't a one-size-fits-all-organizations project management system. Some organizations can find it very challenging to successfully adopt Agile for several reasons.

For one, an organization culture or structure may not be fit for adopting Agile. As mentioned earlier, Agile is built upon flexibility and the ability to welcome change with open arms.

Organizations who have a culture of rigidity and a strong sense of loyalty to traditional ways of doing things aren't cut out for the Agile system.

Having a couple of teams fit for Agile adoption won't cut it - it has to be the whole organization because at some point, non-Agile capable collaborators can be a stumbling block for those that are Agile-compliant.

Everybody from the project teams to sponsors, executives, and leaders must be Agile-friendly.

Another reason why some organizations won't be able to successfully adopt Agile is a poor understanding of general business goals. Adopting Agile for managing projects just won't cut it if the overall goals of an organization aren't clear because even the most effective methods can't accomplish goals that aren't clear to begin with. It's like aiming at an unidentified target. Strategic arrangement is very important for Agile PMS to work.

Another reason why Agile may not work for an organization is rushing the sprints or testing cycles unnecessarily.

When project management teams are more concerned with finishing on time or even earlier than schedule, the risks of overlooking important aspects of sprints or testing cycles are substantially higher, which can have huge negative impacts on projects and ultimately, the whole organization.

By trying to rush projects, the risks for undetected deficiencies or errors are significantly raised.

The last reason why organizations aren't suited for implementing Agile, regardless of how useful it may be, is lack of Agile implementation skills. While the Agile project management system is one of the world's fastest growing systems, the number of professionals who are adept at it aren't growing at the same rate, making qualified and competent Agile practitioners very hard to find.

As such, many organizations simply don't have Agile-abled people to help adopt the system successfully.

Chapter 3 - Agile Software Development Techniques

There are several different ways to apply the Agile PMS to software development, each with its own nuances. We'll discuss them in this chapter.

Scrum Methodology

This refers to a light version of the Agile PMS, which has a wide range of applications for controlling and managing all types of incremental and iterative projects.

Because of its simplicity, established effectiveness, and capability for embracing many engineering practices of other Agile methodologies, Scrum is immensely popular in the Agile world.

Under this methodology, the owner of the product or service being worked on closely collaborates with the software development team so that system functionalities can be identified and prioritized in the form of what's called "product backlogs."

The product backlogs consist of all things required for successful delivery of a working version of software, e.g., non-functional requirements, bug fixes, and product features, among others.

The product owner provides the cross-functional teams involved with the development of a particular software system with priorities that need to be pursued for the project.

The cross functional teams, on the other hand, estimate and commit to give the owner potentially deliverable increments of the software in question during what's known as successive sprints or testing cycles, which normally last an average of 30 days. After the teams commit a specific sprint's product backlogs, additional functionalities may no longer be added to the sprint except those made by the cross-functional teams concerned.

And after the teams have delivered a sprint to the product owner, the product backlog is evaluated and re-prioritized - if needed - and the next batch of functionalities are then selected for inclusion in the succeeding sprints.

This methodology has a proven track record of successful scaling across multiple teams within very big organizations of more than 800 people.

Lean Methodology

An iterative methodology based on the Agile system that was conceptualized by Tom and Mary Poppendieck, the Lean Software Development methodology is primarily grounded on the practices and principles of a movement that was practiced by top companies like Toyota, which is called the Lean Enterprise Movement.

This software development methodology specializes in giving value to customers by focusing on what's referred to as the "value stream," which is the means by which value is provided. Its key principles include:
  – Building integrity;
  – Delivering products and services at the earliest possible time;
  – Emboldening project management teams;

- Learning amplification;
- Looking at the big picture;
- Making decisions at the latest possible time; and
- Waste elimination.

In order to get rid of as much waste as possible, the Lean methodology only chooses features that are really important for a system, gives priority to those chosen features and delivers them to customers in small increments or batches.

The Lean methodology puts a premium on a workflow development's speed and efficiency and depends on a fast and reliable flow of information between stakeholders/customers and software development teams.

It also operates from the perspective that projects' products or services can be pulled upon request of customers.

Lean centers its attention on both the authority and capability for making decisions of small teams and individual members. This is because studies have shown this to be much more efficient and effective compared to traditional and hierarchical control structures.

This Agile methodology also focuses on how efficiently project teams can use resources and ensuring that all members of such teams are optimally productive.

The Lean methodology sets its sights on concurrent jobs as well as on the least amount of potential dependencies among project teams. And finally, the Lean methodology highly suggests using written automated tests simultaneously with the writing of software code.

Kanban Methodology

This methodology is primarily used by organizations to manage product creation processes, emphasizing continuous delivery without imposing unbearable burdens on the cross-functional teams involved. Similar to the Scrum methodology, Kanban seeks to enable teams to collaborate much better.

There are 3 principles upon which the Kanban methodology is founded. These are:

1. Visualization of the workflow, i.e., seeing how all items of the project can provide important information within context of each other;

2. Limited volume of WIP or work-in-progress, which provides the necessary balance to a flows-based software development approach to minimize the chances of project teams starting and committing to too much work all at once;

3. Enhanced workflow, where the next highest priority work item in the backlog gets worked on as soon as something has been successfully completed.

The Kanban Methodology works by encouraging non-stop collaboration as well as continuous and active learning and improvement by identifying the optimal workflow for teams.

Extreme Programming (XP) Methodology

XP has become one of the world's most popular - and controversial - Agile methodologies, which was originally founded on 4 simple values, which are simplicity, feedback, courage, and communications. It's also grounded on 12 important practices, which include:

- Collective ownership of codes;
- Development driven by multiple testings;
- Incremental releases;
- Metaphor;
- Non-stop integration;
- Planning game;
- Programming in pairs;
- Refactoring;
- Simplicity in design;
- Standards for coding;
- Sustainable work rate; and
- Testing for customer acceptance.

XP favors a high degree of involvement or collaboration from customers, fast feedback mechanisms, non-stop testing, non-stop planning, and closely-knit teams for giving customers working versions of software frequently within 1 to 3-week intervals. With XP, customers work tightly with project teams to identify and prioritize "user stories," i.e., very small units of a software's functionalities.

Under this collaboration, the software development teams assess, strategize and deliver the functionalities with the highest priorities in working and tested forms of software in incremental bits.

For optimal productivity, a supportive and lightweight framework is needed to guide the software development teams and ultimately, ensure software of very high quality.

Crystal Methodology

This Agile methodology is a very adaptable and lightweight approach for developing software. The Crystal methodology is made up of a group of Agile methodologies like Crystal Clear, Crystal Orange, and Crystal Yellow, among many others.

These methodologies unique qualities are determined by many factors like a project's priorities, system criticality, and the size of the project team or teams. The Crystal family of methodology works on tailored sets of practices, policies, and processes for each project so that their unique characteristics can be met.

Some of Crystal's key tenets include simplicity, communication, and teamwork. It also includes frequent evaluation to enable teams to continuously adjust and improve processes.

As with other Agile-based methodologies, timely and regular delivery of working versions of software, adaptability, high involvement of end users in the development process, and elimination of distractions or red tape that can bog down development processes are highlighted under the Crystal methodology.

Feature-Driven Development (FDD) Methodology

The earlier versions of this Agile methodology were borne out of collaboration between Peter Coad, who is an OOD authority, and Jeff De Luca. FDD is an iteration process that's short and mostly driven by models and starts with laying a project's general model shape as a foundation.

It then proceeds through several 2-week series of feature and design-based iterations. Such features are incremental, i.e., small, results that are effective or useful from the perspective of clients.

The FDD design process is mostly built around the goal of delivering useful features, which are accomplished through the following activities:

- — Modeling of the domain object;
- — Feature-based development;
- — Ownership of Components or Classes;
- — Establishment of feature teams;
- — Conducting regular inspections;
- — Managing configurations;
- — Building regularly; and
- — Making progresses and results visible.

Under the FDD methodology, specific practices like ownership of components and classes, and building regularly are highly recommended. The people behind FDD say that compared to other approaches or methodologies, it can scale more directly and as such, it's a better fit for teams with much bigger sizes.

And compared to other Agile methodologies, Feature-Driven Development depicts very brief and particular phases of work that will be completed separately according to features which include promote to build, code inspection, code, design inspection, design, and domain walkthrough.

Dynamic Systems Development Method (DSDM)

Finally, this methodology refers to an organized and commonsense driven process that prioritizes fast and efficient delivery of business solutions to clients.

In many different ways, it is comparable to XP and Scrum, but its single best advantage over the two is it's the best methodology where timelines are fixed.

Instead of simply focusing on development teams' activities, DSDM makes the delivery of solutions to its client its primary focus. This methodology does what's necessary to make sure that every project's business sense and feasibility have been established prior to designing and implementing.

Collaboration and cooperation among all stakeholders are emphasized under the Dynamic Systems Development Method, and to make sure all those who are concerned have a very clear idea of all the important aspects of a particular system, it conducts a lot of prototyping.

DSDM grew because of the need for a standardized framework for delivering projects for a popular project development methodology during the early 1990s, which was called Rapid Application Development or RAD. Despite RAD's massive popularity during those times, its software delivery methodologies were lacking in structure.

Because of a lack of such structure, The DSDM Consortium was born and assembled in 1994 for the purpose of coming up with and promoting a standardized or structured rapid software delivery system for the industry. And since then, DDM - as an Agile project management methodology - has morphed and grown into a comprehensive and iterative Agile project planning, management, execution, and scaling methodology for developing software.

This methodology is grounded on 9 important principles that are built around business needs: high user involvement; team empowerment;

frequent delivery; assimilated testing; and collaborations with stakeholders. These 9 principles are:

1. Active involvement of end-users;
2. Empowered project teams;
3. Repeated releasing and updating of iterations;
4. Business needs-driven software development processes;
5. Incremental developments;
6. Acceptance of change;
7. High level of initial requirements;
8. Efficient integration of testing and development, with emphasis on creation of small teams with very good communications among teams and members of such teams; and
9. Putting great importance on cooperation and collaboration among stakeholders.

While the Dynamic Systems Development Method is one that is perfectly capable of being implemented by itself, it can also work well other Agile methods like eXtreme Programming (XP).

DSDM Benefits

Using DSDM as a primary Agile project management system can provide significant benefits to any organization. These include:

- Swiftly and directly visible development results;

- High end-user acceptance of developed systems because of their significant active participation in the development process, which gives them a sense of ownership over such systems;

- Swift delivery of basic features or functionalities, and regular delivery - at intervals - of additional ones;

- Minimal, if any, communications barrier between stakeholders because of minimal or no bureaucracy;

- Much higher chances of developing systems that meet clients' needs, or even exceed them, because of regular communications with end users and frequent receipt of feedback from the same;

- The ability to evaluate whether a project will be able to successfully meet or exceed clients' needs and expectations early in the development process instead of having to wait for having a significant portion of the development completed before being able to do so;

- Timely and cost-efficient delivery or systems and solutions;

- End users have the opportunity to steer systems development in directions that are best aligned with their interests.

In the next chapter, we'll take a look at what's possibly the most popular version or variant of the DSDM - Atern.

Chapter 4 - DSDM Atern

The Dynamic Systems Development Method or DSDM is possibly the most senior Agile methodology around, being launched in 1995 and as such, is the only Agile methodology that concentrates on managing Agile projects.

Over the years, DSDM continued to evolve and the latest model or evolved version of this Agile methodology is Atern, which is an Agile project delivery framework that provides timely delivery of needed solutions to clients.

Atern - as a project management methodology - is able to do this because Atern project teams operate under the guidance of 8 key principles, which are:

1. *Concentration On Business Needs*: Each decision made in every project must be done so with clear ideas of a particular project's main goal, i.e., what the client needs to have delivered, and when such needs need to be delivered. It's crucial to keep in mind that the project itself is not the be-all-and-end-all but simply a means to achieve a goal, which is meeting clients' needs.

2. *Timely Delivery*: Often, timely delivery of products is considered to be the most important factor when it comes to successful completion of projects because in many instances, late delivery can render the development of projects practically useless, most especially when strict legal deadlines and fleeting business opportunities are involved.

3. *Collaboration*: Teams whose members are highly committed and actively cooperate with each other will always trump a team of loosely connected members. With high levels of collaboration

come better understanding, faster completion of tasks, and a strong sense of accountability and project ownership that can result in a high level of member synergy.

4. *No Compromise On Quality*: Under the Atern method, the expected quality level of systems for development and eventual delivery are established from the get go. With a clear expectation of quality for delivery, all efforts are geared towards achieving - or even exceeding - the expected quality level. In other words, solutions developed under the Atern methodology must be at least "good enough" based on clients' expressed needs and quality expectations.

5. *Firm Foundations For Incremental Development*: Atern is big on incremental delivery, i.e., delivery of solutions in smaller but more frequent iterations. The reason for this is simple: early delivery of real and practical business benefits. Incremental delivery makes stakeholders, especially the end-users, confident about the solutions being developed because of their regular feedback to developers, and leads to better succeeding iterations because of such feedback. With regular deployment of incremental builds, clients have the opportunity to much more quickly enjoy the benefits of solutions being developed instead of having to wait to receive the entire solution in one big, final version. And incremental delivery - with feedback from end-users for every increment - provides information that can help make succeeding iterations even better.

6. *Iterations-Based Development Of Solutions*: Using an iterative approach to developing business solutions allows Atern teams to provide solutions that are able to accurately meet end-user customers' needs. The concept of iteration is nestled throughout any Atern project's life cycle. It's unusual for systems or solutions to be perfectly built and get everything

right just on the first try or delivery and practically all projects experience change in one way or another. In order to effectively ride the waves of change and to be able to come up with optimally effective solutions, the Atern methodology encourages an iteration-reliant and realistic approach to dealing with changes. Through this, the Atern methodology is able to ensure that solutions developed will be able to meet clients' needs.

7. *Clear And Continuous Communications*: In most cases, projects fail because of horrible communications between team members, teams, and stakeholders. Techniques used in the Atern methodology were particularly made with the intention of - among others - to make communications more free flowing, unimpeded, clear, and effective not just among teams but most especially among individuals. Through things like Stand-ups and Facilitated Workshops, user involvement in the development processes, and clearly defined roles, Atern emphasizes the importance of human interactions, which can often be much more effective at getting things done optimally compared to largely textual communications with very little or no human interactions.

8. *Exercise Of Control*: For any project to be successfully completed, team leaders must exercise a great degree of control. Within an Atern environment, teams have to be proactive instead of reactive when it comes to progress monitoring and control. Otherwise, things may not go as planned or worse, get out of hand.

Project Variables

Projects usually have four parameters within which they're managed: quality, features, cost, and time. It would be impractical or unrealistic to ensure all parameters are fixed from the get go. In fact, doing so is one of reasons why many projects encounter delays or worse, bog down and don't get completed.

For example, only the features of a solution are fixed when it comes to traditional or non-Agile project management systems, while cost and time are considered to be variable. Thus, additional resources or extensions to project delivery times are required when projects go off track.

But here's the thing: merely adding more resources to a project that's already late only makes it, well, later! From a business and credibility perspective, unmet project deadlines can be fatal. At this point, quality can also be affected, making it variable factor as well that's dependent on cost, delivery, and late delivery.

But such isn't the case when using an Atern project management methodology, which is able to address the quality, cost, and time issues during the Foundations Phase and the issue of contingency is managed well by tweaking a to-be-delivered solution feature. And as is the case when contingency measures are needed, lower or low priority features may be removed or postponed upon the express agreement of everyone concerned in order to successfully and promptly deliver solutions. In the end, Atern projects will always be able to deliver working solutions.

Suitable Levels Of Formality

At the core, the Atern project management methodology needs to identify the appropriate levels of formality or rigor for every project because no two projects are the same. If there's so much rigor or formality, it's highly possible for projects to be slowed down unnecessarily or worse, get stuck.

Very little rigor or formality can result in a very loose or spontaneous approach to solutions development that foster a working environment of no urgency, which can lead to regular procrastinations and eventually, delays.

The key is to identify the suitable level of formality for every project, just enough to ensure projects won't get "out of governance" and foster progress, not hinder it.

Chapter 5 - Roles In DSDM Project Management

When it comes to applying a DSDM project management methodology, there are many different roles that need to be played and filled up by different but capable people.

These roles can be grouped by interest and by actual responsibilities or function. The following are the various interest-based roles in DSDM:

- Business-oriented roles, i.e., business perspective or expertise;

- Technical or solution-oriented roles, i.e., technical perspective or expertise;

- Leadership or management-oriented roles, i.e., leadership and general management skills or perspective;

- Process-oriented roles, i.e., process definition and monitoring perspective or expertise.

Next are the 13 specific roles played under a DSDM project management methodology. Keep in mind that DSDM's key principles are generally focused on communications and collaboration. An efficient working team of capable individuals are at the core of successful DSDM projects.

Remember, the most effective solutions are borne of empowered and self-organizing teams.

And before going into each specific DSDM role, keep in mind 3 important factors that can substantially influence any such project's success rate, which are mutual respect among all team members, commitment and accountability for work responsibilities, and continuous improvements in the way team members work together. So without further ado, here are the 13 roles team members of a DSDM project need to fill:

1. Business Sponsor: At the project level, this is the highest role or position. Because of their business-focused interest, their commitment to any project, proposed solutions, and means by which to achieving them are unquestionable. They are accountable for both the project's budget and business case.

2. Business Visionary: As the name suggests, this role is responsible for giving the project its vision, identifying the project sponsor's needs, identifying the end-users of a solution being developed through the project, communicating such information to all team members, and giving the team instructions to follow for successfully completing a project. And to avoid role inconsistencies or duplications, it's best to assign this role to just one person.

3. Technical Coordinator: This role is primarily responsible for coming up with solutions that are congruent with the clients' needs, ensuring that people that fill up technical roles are adequately skilled, and making sure that the technical people are working properly. This is the technical equivalent of the previous role, the Business Visionary.

4. Project Manager: Aside from giving leadership to the DSDM project team in accordance with Agile PMS principles, people who fill up this role are primarily responsible for managing the solution development team's working environment. Being the coordinator and facilitator of a project, they are responsible for assigning the scale and details of problems that may potentially

arise in their team, which may be beyond the decision-making authority of the team.

5. Business Analyst: People who fill up this role are the only ones with multiple interests, i.e., they have sufficient knowledge of both the business needs of the project and the technical solutions that can meet the end-users' functional and non-functional requirements. Typically, business analysts belong to a Solutions Development group and are deployed at the level of projects.

6. Team Leader: Those who occupy this role have the responsibility of making development teams optimally productive, functioning as the service leader. It's somewhat akin to a Scrum Master role, in that people occupying this role preferably should be selected by work colleagues within the respective Solutions Development Teams as well as be the team's meetings facilitators.

7. Business Ambassador: People who fill up this role act as the development teams' key business representatives, particularly in the areas of prioritization and creation of requirements during the foundations and feasibility stages. Business ambassadors are responsible for every detail and prioritization in the development process. The role of business ambassador is akin to a product owner's in that it requires making business decisions for development teams.

8. Solutions Developer: People occupying this role are competent and able to improve or expand solutions by identifying and converting requirements effectively in order to ensure that all of the client's business and technical needs are met. Solutions developers function similarly to a Scrum team member, but

they have skills that are more concentrated on solutions or software development.

9. Solutions Tester: Because the DSDM methodology highlights clear definition and assurance of a specific level of quality, people occupying this role are responsible not just for identifying but also for conducting tests in accordance with an agreed upon strategy. Like the solutions developer, the solutions tester role is akin to that of a Scrum team members except that this role requires skills that are more focused on solutions testing.

10. Business Advisor: People who fill this role provide support to the team by way of business specific expertise and knowledge that other project or development team members do not possess. Business advisors are considered as subject matter experts on the business side of projects and may represent compliance or legal aspects that need to be taken into consideration, focus groups, or end-users.

11. Technical Advisor: People filling up this role have responsibilities similar to those of business advisors except that such responsibilities are geared more towards the technical areas of solutions development. Examples of such responsibilities include having extensive know-how of the technology utilized in the project, providing technical support, and identification and meeting of production or development requirements, among others.

12. Workshop Facilitator: DSDM recommends several key practices, which include workshops. People who fill the role of workshop facilitators need to be neutral, i.e., taking neither the side of end-users nor the development or project teams, and

must have the ability to facilitate workshops among people of different backgrounds and attitudes very well.

13. The Coach (DSDM Coach): Adopting specific processes and mindsets necessary for transitioning into an Agile framework can be very challenging, the latter being the most challenging. In general, people who fill up this role are responsible for helping project teams deal with these challenges in order to make the successful transition to an Agile framework. Basically, think of what NBA coaches Steve Kerr of Golden State Warrior dynasty and Brad Stevens of the young and overachieving Boston Celtics do, except think of it within an Agile PMS context.

Don't be surprised that despite the many roles that need to be filled in DSDM project management teams, some people may occupy multiple roles and assuming all the relevant responsibilities of those roles, especially in relatively small or young project teams.

Also, don't be surprised to find that some roles aren't around for the entire project's duration. Some supporting roles will only need to be activated as needs arise.

Chapter 6 - Managing Scope And Procurement With Agile

Any project management discussion wouldn't be complete without a discussion on project scope and procurement of supplies.

Two of the things that make the Agile project management system very popular and effective are its approach to project scoping and procurement.

Agile Project Scoping

One way to see why agile project scoping is better than traditional ways of doing it is to talk about traditional project management. In the past, bulk of the work comprising project management is scope management.

When talking about product or solution requirements and features, the discussion focuses on product scope, which is basically all work required to create a product or solution.

Dynamic or changing product requirements are perceived as "failures" in terms of planning per traditional project management. But as you may have remembered from our earlier discussions, Agile project management systems think of changes as means by which to come up with even better products or solutions because the Agile PMS employs variable scoping, unlike traditional project management systems that employ static scoping.

The great minds behind the Agile Manifesto saw that not only are changing scopes natural but that they're also beneficial. In short, an

Agile project management methodology do not shun or vilify changes but rather embrace them as allies or BFFs (best friends forever) in the battle for quality and effective products and solutions.

If traditional project management views changing requirements during development as failures, an Agile project with no changes in requirements along the way that can lead to learning something useful about how to make products or solutions even better is considered a failed one.

In fact, Agile projects are expected to have frequently changing backlogs as a result of free-flowing feedback between development teams and end-users because development teams don't know everything about projects in the beginning.

And the Agile project management systems - including its Manifesto and key operating principles - give teams an idea of how agile they really are. That's why the extent to which project approaches are in line with the Agile manifesto is the extent of an adopted project management methodology's "agility."

While Agile projects are still ongoing, new product requirements can be identified by just about any stakeholder, e.g., end-users, the product owner, the Scrum team, etc.

In particular, the product owner identifies new requirements and assigns value and priority to them vis-a-vis existing ones in a product's backlog.

"Scope Creep" is a term that's very popular within traditional project management circles and is used to refer to requirements that undergo a change after the initial definition stage has already been concluded.

Because traditional project management approaches like the Waterfall technique are highly rigid, they aren't able to positively deal with or include changing requirements once projects, which are already underway. As such, changes in requirement or scope often lead to schedule and budget problems in projects. If you bring up "scope creep" in any conversations with a traditional or Waterfall-centered project manager, don't be surprised to see him or her cringe or shudder at the thought.

But such isn't the case with Agile. Because of its - pardon the pun - agility, Agile teams can use initial or existing product backlogs to evaluate whether or not newly identified requirements are worthy enough to be included in succeeding sprints.

And in situations where newly identified requirements are deemed worthy, existing but least-priority requirements may either remain in the backlog for future reconsideration or be completely removed from it.

When it comes to scope management, the following Agile principles are the most relevant:
- Principle #1: The highest priority is customer satisfaction via continuous and early delivery of important software;

- Principle #2: Changes in requirements are welcome, even in the latter stages of development because Agile processes can utilize such changes to give its customers distinct competitive advantages;

- Principle #3: Frequent delivery of working versions of important software, which can be anywhere from every few weeks to every few months, with a shorter timeframe being more preferred;

− Principle #10: Simplicity is essential, i.e., the ability to optimize an amount of work that's not performed.

In summary, the following are the ways by which the Agile approach to project scoping is superior to the traditional approach to managing products:

1. Product owners identify top-priority requirements at the start of every project and breaks them down in greater detail to identify those that need to be implemented in the short-term. As project teams get to know their customers more and as their projects grow, they identify and refine project requirements throughout the entire project life span.

2. Organizations can look at changing requirements in a positive light, i.e., as means by which to make products even better during the project development stage. And often, it's the changes during the latter stages of a project that can provide the most value because of the accumulated knowledge about a product at such a point in a product's development stage.

3. Managing changing requirements is an intrinsic part of any Agile project management process, and it gives development teams the opportunities for continuous scope assessment and for incorporating newly identified requirements in every sprint. The value and rank of new requirements are determined by product owners, who also adds the new requirements to a product's backlog.

4. Because schedule and resources fixing is only done initially, additional and very important features won't necessarily ruin a project's schedule or budget in an Agile project. Important and newly-added features will only bump off or push the least-important priorities or features out of the way because an

iterative approach to development - one that Agile projects have - gives leeway for making changes to a product's backlog with every sprint.

5. Particularly in Scrum teams, a project's scope is determined through consideration of features that have a direct contribution to the project's sprint goal, release goal, and vision. To guarantee that the highest-value features are included in the product and are delivered to clients as soon as possible, development teams focus on creating highest-value features first.

Agile Procurement

An Agile project management methodology approaches procurement differently from traditional project management. Procurement, as with scope, is considered to be a part of a project's investment side because it involves managing the purchase or procurement of necessary supplies or services for successfully accomplishing a project's scope.

Under the Agile Manifesto, collaboration with customers takes a higher priority over negotiation of contracts with them. And this provides a good context for developing good relationships with suppliers for Agile projects. But this doesn't mean Agile projects don't use contracts for the procurement process. It can never be as negotiations and contracts are crucial aspects of any business relationship, regardless of how good or bad such relationships are.

It's just that in Agile-managed projects, teams would rather develop very good working relationships with suppliers and customers instead of having to squabble over unimportant details and removing items in contracts that may not necessarily be important.

When it comes to the procurement process, all 12 principles of the Agile PMS are applicable. But, the following seem to be more relevant than the rest when it comes to this part of project management:

- Principle #2: Changes in requirements are welcome, even in the latter stages of development because Agile processes can utilize such changes to give its customers' distinct competitive advantages;

- Principle #3: Frequent delivery of working versions of important software, which can be anywhere from every few weeks to every few months, with a shorter timeframe being more preferred;

- Principle #4: All throughout the project, it's important for business people and the software developers to work closely together every day;

- Principle #5: Motivated members are crucial for building projects successfully, that's why it's important to provide project teams with a working environment, everything they may need to successfully build projects, and a high level of trust that they'll get things done;

- Principle #10: Simplicity is essential, i.e., the ability to optimize the amount of work that's not performed;

- Principle #11: Self-organized teams can give the best project architectures, requirements, and designs.

To have a better idea of how an Agile PMS is superior to traditional project management systems when it comes to managing procurement, consider the following:

1. An Agile approach to procurement is one where self-managing or organizing development teams have a much bigger participation in identifying those that need to be procured for successfully building projects, where the Scrum master is responsible for the actual acquisition of items needed for the team;

2. Agile projects use contracts that aren't based on unchangeable documented deliverables that may not be helpful in terms of helping development teams create quality products but are based on working functionalities at the conclusion of every sprint.

3. Agile PMS teams concentrate on fostering and maintaining good working relationships between sellers and buyers at the inception of each procurement process;

4. At the conclusion of each sprint, vendors deliver completely working functionalities and if there's a change in vendors midway through any project, new vendors would be able to quickly develop requirements for succeeding sprints without the need for costly and extended transitions.

While both Agile PMS and Waterfall-based development teams want their vendors to succeed, they deal with them differently.

Waterfall or traditional teams concentrate too much on compliance from and accountability of vendors, where vendors are judged by their ability to check off deliverables and documents from a list.

Agile teams on the other hand, are more focused on end results and base their successes on their ability to deliver working functionalities.

Conclusion

Thank you for buying this book. I hope that through this book, I wasn't just able to help you learn more about the Agile project management system but also to encourage you to take action on what you learned.

After all, knowledge without application is merely trivia and the knowledge can only become "power" after application. Without it, knowledge is powerless and consequently, worthless.

So how can you act on what you learned here? Well, the best way is to read more advanced materials on Agile or attend classes or courses that can help you get certified as a professional Agile project management practitioner.

And more than just getting certified, such classes or courses like the ones I enumerated in Chapter 2 can provide you with very comprehensive training on the subject matter, both on a theoretical and a practical level.

So here's to your success as an Agile project management practitioner my friend! Cheers!

References:

1. https://www.cio.com/article/3156998/agile-development/agile-project-management-a-beginners-guide.html
2. https://www.cio.com/article/3201284/certifications/7-agile-certifications-to-take-your-career-to-the-next-level.html
3. http://agilemanifesto.org/
4. https://www.smartsheet.com/comprehensive-guide-values-principles-agile-manifesto
5. https://www.versionone.com/agile-101/agile-methodologies/
6. http://www.quotium.com/performance/9-principles-building-blocks-dsdm-agile/
7. http://www.mcpa.biz/2011/08/what-is-dsdm-atern/
8. https://www.agilebusiness.org/content/atern-principles
9. https://www.netmind.net/knowledge-center/roles-and-responsibilities-in-the-dsdm-agile-project-framework/
10. http://www.dummies.com/careers/project-management/whats-different-agile-procurement/
11. http://www.dummies.com/careers/project-management/whats-different-agile-scope-management/
12. https://www.linkedin.com/pulse/5-phases-agile-trevor-a-stasik
13. https://developer.epa.gov/guide/templates-guides/agile/performance-measurement/